Cairns & Great Barrier Reef
Travel Guide

Quick Trips Series

No part of this publication may be reproduced, stored in a retrieval system, or transmitted, in any form or by any means without the prior written permission of the publisher, nor be otherwise circulated in any form of binding or cover other than that in which it is published and without similar condition being imposed on the subsequent purchaser. If there are any errors or omissions in copyright acknowledgements the publisher will be pleased to insert the appropriate acknowledgement in any subsequent printing of this publication. Although we have taken all reasonable care in researching this book we make no warranty about the accuracy or completeness of its content and disclaim all liability arising from its use.

Copyright © 2016, Astute Press
All Rights Reserved.

Table of Contents

CAIRNS & THE GREAT BARRIER REEF 6
- Ecology & Marine Life 8
- Geography 9

SIGHTS & ACTIVITIES: WHAT TO SEE & DO 12
- Cairns 12
- Cairns Night Zoo Safari 14
- Green Island 16
- Great Barrier Reef Pontoon & Knuckle Reef Lagoon 17
- Daintree Rainforest Tour 19
- Kuranda Scenic Railway 20
- Atherton Tablelands 22
- Port Douglas 25
- Fitzroy Island 27
- Cape Tribulation 29
- Cape York 31
- Tully River White Water Rafting 32
- Aboriginal Cultural Tjapukai Tour 34

BUDGET TIPS 37

- 🌐 **ACCOMMODATION** 37
  - Cairns Coconut Holiday Resort 37
  - Tropical Heritage Cairns 38
  - Atherton Hinterland Motel 39
  - Port Douglas Motel 39
- 🌐 **RESTAURANTS, CAFÉS & BARS** 40
  - Bayleaf Balinese Restaurant 40
  - Houdini's Gourmet Pizza 41
  - Grill'd 42
  - Devine Gelato 43
- 🌐 **SHOPPING** 43
  - The Pier 43
  - Cairns Central 44

KNOW BEFORE YOU GO — 45

- 🌐 ENTRY REQUIREMENTS 45
- 🌐 HEALTH INSURANCE 45
- 🌐 TRAVELLING WITH PETS 46
- 🌐 AIRPORTS 48
- 🌐 AIRLINES 50
- 🌐 HUBS 52
- 🌐 MONEY MATTERS 52
- 🌐 CURRENCY 52
- 🌐 BANKING/ATMS 53
- 🌐 CREDIT CARDS 53
- 🌐 TOURIST TAX 54
- 🌐 CLAIMING BACK VAT 54
- 🌐 TIPPING POLICY 55
- 🌐 CONNECTIVITY 56

Mobile Phones	56
🌐 Dialling Code	57
🌐 Emergency Numbers	57
🌐 General Information	57
🌐 Public Holidays	57
🌐 Time Zones	58
🌐 Daylight Savings Time	59
🌐 School Holidays	59
🌐 Trading Hours	60
🌐 Driving Policy	60
🌐 Drinking Policy	61
🌐 Smoking Policy	62
🌐 Electricity	62
🌐 Food & Drink	63
🌐 Useful Websites	65

CAIRNS & THE GREAT BARRIER REEF TRAVEL GUIDE

Cairns & the Great Barrier Reef

Australia's Great Barrier Reef is one of the seven natural wonders of the world and is often showcased in magazines like *National Geographic* and *Travel and Leisure*. One of the world's best and most accessible coral reefs, the Great Barrier Reef is also the only natural structure on earth that is visible from outer space. Located off the coast of Queensland, it has 2,900 individual coral

CAIRNS & THE GREAT BARRIER REEF TRAVEL GUIDE

reefs and over 900 islands covering 2,600 sq. km, making it the planet's largest UNESCO World Heritage site.

Cairns is located close to the Great Barrier Reef and the Daintree Rainforest. It is the gateway to the region and attracts snorkelers, scuba divers, cruise ship visitors, and fishing enthusiasts.

However, Cairns is a destination in it's own right and attracts rainforest walkers, native bird watchers, wildlife explorers and others. It is an intimate cosmopolitan city that has spectacular scenery, first rate accommodation, culture and art. Tourism Australia rates Cairns as the fourth most popular travel destination for international travellers to Australia.

CAIRNS & THE GREAT BARRIER REEF TRAVEL GUIDE

Whether you are looking for a relaxing break or adventurous thrills, Cairns and the Great Barrier Reef will deliver. Located in this vibrant tropical paradise, the area comes complete with a variety of festivals and events.

🌎 Ecology & Marine Life

The Great Barrier Reef is home to several endangered species of flora and fauna, many of which are native to the reef. Famous for its diverse marine life, the Great Barrier Reef is home to over 1,500 species of fish, 5,000 types of mollusc, 400 sponges and over 300 types of coral. The reef is also the breeding site for six species of sea turtles including the loggerhead sea turtle and the leatherback sea turtle. In addition, thirty types of dolphins, whales, and porpoises have also been seen around the reef. You might even see a humpback whale, humpback dolphin or a dwarf minke whale. Cairns is home to the

CAIRNS & THE GREAT BARRIER REEF TRAVEL GUIDE

Cassowary, considered to be the world's most dangerous bird. The Hercules, Australia's largest moth, measuring 25 cms in wingspan is also mainly found here.

Since 1985, the Great Barrier Reef has lost over 50% of its coral from a variety of environmental issues. The Reef has suffered from pollution, oil spills, ocean warming and tropical cyclones. The Australian and Queensland governments are working hard to offset the damage to the ecosystem. There's still much to see.

🌍 Geography

Located on the eastern coastline of the Cape York Peninsula in the state of Queensland in Northeastern Australia, Cairns is situated on a coastal strip between the Great Dividing Range and the Coral Sea. The Cairns International Airport is situated between the Cairns CBD

CAIRNS & THE GREAT BARRIER REEF TRAVEL GUIDE

and its beaches on the coast. Among the top ten fastest growing towns of Australia, Cairns attracts more than 4 million international and domestic passengers making the Cairns International Airport the seventh busiest domestic airport and the sixth busiest international airport in Australia.

Cairns railway station is the terminus of Queensland's North Coast railway which travels up the Queensland coast from Brisbane. Cairns is also the starting point for the Kuranda Scenic Railway, a popular tourist train that winds its way through the Macalister Range, passing through the suburbs of Stratford, Freshwater, and Redlynch before arriving at Kuranda.

Coaches are an alternate mode of travel that link Cairns to Brisbane and cities to the south. Additionally, Cairns

CAIRNS & THE GREAT BARRIER REEF TRAVEL GUIDE

has a well-connected public bus network – the Marlin Coast Sunbus. Other forms of transport include mini bus and the Cairns taxi service.

Cairns Seaport is the main port for tourists embarking on reef trips. Catamarans of varied sizes – from small ones that take about 12 tourists to huge ones taking on board more than 300 passengers – conduct daily tours and trips. The seaport is also a stopover for cruise ships as well as providing freight services to other coastal towns. Climate & When to Visit Cairns and the Great Barrier Reef have a tropical monsoon climate. November to May is the wet season when tropical monsoons hit the city often causing flooding of the Mulgrave and Barron rivers. Monsoons during these months can also affect road and rail access in the city. The months of June through October are drier,

CAIRNS & THE GREAT BARRIER REEF TRAVEL GUIDE

although frequent showers are common. Summers are hot and humid while winters are warm.

Air and water temperatures in Cairns and the Great Barrier Reef range from the low 70s to mid-80s Fahrenheit all year round. Although Queensland's lukewarm waters are ideal for diving all through the year, the best time to visit Cairns and the Great Barrier Reef are the months of June through November. During this period, diving visibility is at its best and the winter weather is generally mild. The summer months (December to March) is the monsoon season and has high humidity and high rainfall.

CAIRNS & THE GREAT BARRIER REEF TRAVEL GUIDE

Sights & Activities: What to See & Do

 Cairns

http://www.cairns-greatbarrierreef.org.au/places/cairns.aspx

The gateway to the Great Barrier Reef, Cairns, is a small yet modern city complete with esplanades, parks and

CAIRNS & THE GREAT BARRIER REEF TRAVEL GUIDE

lagoons. Cairns does not have a beach itself but the northern beaches near Cairns are only a short drive away.

Cairns city is an urban jungle of tour operators, souvenir shops, car hire agents and restaurants. For those looking forward to the nightlife, Cairns has nightclubs and bars as well as accommodation and eateries that suit every budget. Waterfront dining along the Cairns Marina offers magnificent views overlooking large boats and the tranquil waterfront esplanade.

Along the 3-kilometer long Foreshore Promenade is a 4,800 square metre saltwater swimming lagoon, an architectural marvel which brings the beach and ocean swimming experience to the heart of the city. The Cairns Night Markets located right opposite the promenade showcase local artworks, tourism trinkets and indigenous

CAIRNS & THE GREAT BARRIER REEF TRAVEL GUIDE

art in addition to serving good food seven days a week. Another spot worth visiting is the Cascade Falls, a series of beautiful waterfalls and pools about 20 kilometers from Cairns. The Quetta Memorial Cathedral located north of Cairns and Cape York is the smallest cathedral in the world.

For those interested in learning about the history of Cairns, the Cairns Museum exhibits offer insights into the famous Cairns-Kuranda Railway, the Chinese temples near to Cairns as well as displays about the goldfields on the Palmer and Hodgkinson rivers.

🌏 Cairns Night Zoo Safari

The Cairns Night Zoo Safari is a fun way to experience nocturnal wildlife. The experience starts at 7 PM when guides from the night zoo greet you at the entrance and

CAIRNS & THE GREAT BARRIER REEF TRAVEL GUIDE

escort you to a BBQ dinner and you can make dietary requests e.g. vegetarian food.

The nocturnal experience gets underway after dinner when you set out to see the animals armed with torches provided by the guides. You can interact with possums and pet koalas on the tour. On a clear night you can stargaze and identify constellations like the Big Dipper or the Southern Cross, so brush up your astronomy in advance.

In the crocodile lair you can see the crocodile's eyes glowing in the darkness. There is a good chance that you will see kangaroos in the wild. At the end of the safari, you get a chance to unwind when complimentary drinks are served. The zoo safari is exciting for children and they can learn the steps of famous Australian bush dances which are performed at the end of the safari. A souvenir shop at the end of the trail gives you an opportunity to purchase memorabilia.

The Cairns Night Zoo Safari costs about $95 per adult and $50 per child. Infants are admitted free of charge and there are no discounted family packages. The Cairns Night Zoo Safari also has packages that include pick up and drop off from Cairns for an added cost. Packages including pick up and drop off cost about $125 per adult and $63 per child.

🌏 Green Island

Named after the astronomer Charles Green, Green Island is a 6,000 year old cay situated 27 kilometers – about 45 minutes –from Cairns. You can choose from an array of activities available on Green Island or just relax and

CAIRNS & THE GREAT BARRIER REEF TRAVEL GUIDE

unwind. Walking around the 1.5 kilometer island takes only about 20 minutes. Snorkeling around the waters of the Green Island is a much sought after activity as it gives you an opportunity to see the marine life of the reef. You can even walk underwater using helmets on a deep sea underwater walk.

The tropical island is a national park and is home to over 100 species of plant life and birds. The beach is an excellent place to relax and you can rent beach furniture along the beach. Typically, the use of 2 chairs and a table costs about $20.

The average price of a Great Barrier Reef exploration tour from the island is about $85 per adult and $40 per child. Family packages cost around $210. Most packages include snorkeling gear, lounge chairs and beach umbrellas as well as activities like feeding the fish and kayaking. Some operators also include activities like deep sea diving and glass bottomed boat tours. Activities like scuba diving and helicopter flights are also available from Green Island.

🌍 Great Barrier Reef Pontoon& Knuckle Reef Lagoon

An ocean site of remarkable possibilities, the Pontoon at the Knuckle Reef Lagoon offers direct access to the Great Barrier Reef. Here, you can explore a wonderland under the water and be awed by the colourful corals and the diversity of marine life. Snorkeling in these waters is an out-of-this-world experience. Queensland's largest and best underwater viewing chambers are here as well. Come to the Knuckle Reef Lagoon to explore the beaches, swim, snorkel, or sail close to the reef. Diving

CAIRNS & THE GREAT BARRIER REEF TRAVEL GUIDE

expeditions come to the Pontoon from Cairns and the towns nearby as well as from the resorts on the Whitsunday Islands.

A World Heritage site since 1981, the Great Barrier Reef is an area of great diversity of flora, fauna and ecology. From the shallow waters along the coastline, the reef stretches 250 kilometers offshore. On some of the cays, you can see breeding colonies of turtles and seabirds.

You can swim, snorkel, sail, and dive on the Great Barrier Reef from the Knuckle Reef Lagoon so hire a pair of flippers and a wet suit and dive right in. Don't miss the opportunity to at least snorkel to see the coral, fish and caves with your family and friends or get more adventurous with a dive instructor. This is one of the best places in the world to see colourful coral and schools of fish underwater.

🌐 Daintree Rainforest Tour

http://www.cairns-greatbarrierreef.org.au/places/daintree.aspx

A tropical rainforest along the northeast coast of Queensland, Daintree Rainforest covers 1,200 square kilometers and is a rare survivor of over 100 million years of climate change. In addition to being the oldest living rainforest on earth, the Daintree Rainforest National Park is also the point where two World Heritage sites – the Great Barrier Reef and the Daintree Rainforest – meet. Accessible through Cape Tribulation or the Mossman Gorge, the Daintree Rainforest is one of the best areas of

CAIRNS & THE GREAT BARRIER REEF TRAVEL GUIDE

natural beauty one could ever encounter. Along the Daintree river is nestled the Daintree Village, where cruise boats glide between natural jungle homes of animals, birds and reptiles. Eco-tourism operators offer exciting itineraries that offer fascinating views and insights into the flora and fauna that inhabit this beautiful river system.

There are various modes of transport available to get to the Daintree Rainforest including rental cars, bus tours, helicopters, planes and boats. However, one should take care in the Daintree Rainforest during the peak monsoon summer season as causeways often get flooded. Guided tours range from $55-$180 per person. Overnight wilderness tours cost more than regular day tours. The travel time from Cairns to the Daintree Rainforest by car is about 2 hours.

🌐 Kuranda Scenic Railway

http://www.ksr.com.au/Pages/Default.aspx

Attracting more than a half-million visitors every year, the Kuranda Scenic Railway is a recommended activity for visitors to Cairns and the Great Barrier Reef. A 90-minute journey, the train makes its way from Cairns to the Kuranda mountain village, passing through the spectacular Barron Gorge National Park. Kuranda Village is home to Bird World, Koala Gardens Wildlife Park, Australian Butterfly Sanctuary, rainforests, bustling village markets and more.

The scenic railway courses through 15 tunnels and over 37 bridges. Along the route, you will see spectacular beauty, steep ravines, deep mountain gorges and valleys, waterfalls and other breathtaking wonders.

CAIRNS & THE GREAT BARRIER REEF TRAVEL GUIDE

Begin your journey at either the Cairns Railway station or from the Freshwater Train Station. Freshwater Train Station is most popular and offers a restaurant with breakfasts and hot coffee takeaways for early morning departures. The station is also home to a Train Museum, a theatre, the Pioneer Cottage and the Kuranda Scenic Railway souvenir shop. The train makes a stop at the Barron Falls railway station overlooking the Barron River, the gorge and the waterfalls. Here passengers can get off the train to take some memorable pictures.

An adult ticket to the Kuranda Skyrail and scenic railway, costs $106 which includes a skyrail trip and the Kuranda Scenic Railway. A children's ticket costs $54 and a family package costs $265. The scenic railway gives passengers an amazing view of the rainforests while the sky rail provides an extraordinary aerial view of the forest. Advance booking is recommended.

Atherton Tablelands

http://www.athertontablelands.com.au/

Known for its mild tropical climate and absence of climactic extremes, the Atherton Tableland has pleasant temperatures ranging between 62 and 77 degrees Fahrenheit in wintertime from July to August. The Tableland enjoys mild, sunny winter days and cool summer nights.

Located 90 kilometers southwest of Cairns, the Tablelands range from 500 meters to 1280 meters above sea level and climactic conditions are very different from those experienced at the coast. Covering an area of 620 square kilometers, the Atherton Tablelands and the Cairns Highlands are home to a number of scenic drives, rainforest walks, boat cruises, giant trees and attractive wildlife. You might come across some of the unique marsupial creatures that are indigenous to Atherton, like the tree kangaroo, musky rat kangaroo, scrub turkey hens and cassowaries.

Two world heritage listed crater lakes – the Eacham and Barrine – are the two blue areas that stand out in a sea of green. If you are in the mood for a picnic, a barbeque lunch or a swim in the deep clear waters, then you should visit Lake Eacham on the Tablelands.

Lake Barrine has a historic teahouse on site and is a good place to visit if you are in the mood for a Devonshire tea. Guided boat tours of Lake Barrine can be arranged at the

CAIRNS & THE GREAT BARRIER REEF TRAVEL GUIDE

teahouse. On the boat tour you may see eels, turtles and various water birds.

Another natural wonder found on the Atherton Tableland is the Mount Hypipamee Crater which formed when escaping natural gases blasted a hole through the solid granite. Located along the Kennedy Highway, about 25 kilometers from Atherton, the Mount Hypipamee National Park has been built around the crater and you will see a rainforest and wildlife as well.

The Atherton Tablelands feature the picturesque Malanda waterfalls that tumble over basalt lava and culminate in the historic Malanda swimming pool. Here, you can enjoy a picnic, a swim or simply a walk through the rainforest.

CAIRNS & THE GREAT BARRIER REEF TRAVEL GUIDE

Another popular swimming spot is near to the MillaaMillaa falls, 3 kilometers from the main highway. The MillaaMillaa falls are surrounded by diverse flora and fauna and you might see a Ulysses butterfly or a platypus here. Iridescent dragonflies perch on shrubs and trees in the rainforest and you can take amazing pictures. Picnic spots, BBQs and parking are accessible to most of the waterfalls in the Atherton Tablelands making visiting them an enjoyable experience.

Atherton can be enjoyed by car or bus. You should drive with caution as it is not unusual to see wildlife crossing the roads or wandering alongside the highway. Self-guided tour information is available from the website.

🌐 Port Douglas

Just 70 kilometers and an hour's drive from Cairns, Port Douglas is well situated for tours to Mossman Gorge and Cape Tribulation. Appealing to those who prefer a more remote atmosphere, Port Douglas is a resort town that is smaller and quieter than Cairns. The outer reef of the Great Barrier Reef is closer to Port Douglas and thus offers visitors the option to visit three different reef sites close by.

You can drive or travel on one the coaches that operate between Cairns and Port Douglas. The average cost of a coach ticket is $35 - $40 per person and family packages are available. Buses leave every 2-3 hours and it is recommended that you confirm timings and pick up points when you book. Advance booking is recommended.

CAIRNS & THE GREAT BARRIER REEF TRAVEL GUIDE

Take a stroll along Macrossan Street, the central hub of Port Douglas. Bikes are available for hire for those interested in cycling by the beach. On Macrossan Street, you will find fine dining, restaurants, cafes and bars, boutique shops, bookstores and more. Prices in Port Douglas can be more expensive than Cairns where the population is higher. Port Douglas also has fewer options for shopping compared to Cairns.

A popular attraction at Port Douglas is the Four Mile Beach. Located at the southern end of the Macrossan Street, it is a palm fringed, white sand beach that is very popular for its spectacular views of sunset. At the inlet end of the Macrossan Street is Anzac Park, home to the chapel St. Mary's by the Sea. If you happen to be here on a Sunday, do not miss the markets where you can pick up some indigenous artwork and charming souvenirs.

The Wildlife Habitat at Port Douglas is another attraction that's worth visiting if you are in the vicinity. Here you will get an opportunity to hand feed and pet koalas, kangaroos, wallabies and cassowaries up close. The Wildlife Habitat is open from 8 AM to 5 PM every day except on Christmas. Adult tickets are priced at $32 per person while a child ticket costs $16. Family tickets can be purchased at $80, standard inclusion being 2 adults and 2 children.

Port Douglas has a serenity and peaceful ambience that draws visitors to the region.

Fitzroy Island

Located 29 kilometers southeast of Cairns, Fitzroy Island is a 45-minute boat trip. With several tour operators running day trips to the island, you will have plenty of

CAIRNS & THE GREAT BARRIER REEF TRAVEL GUIDE

options to choose from. The average cost of a day trip to Fitzroy Island from Cairns is about $60-70 per person. Some tour packages include lunch. Additional activities like visiting the Little Fitzroy Island to view its coral or kayaking, canoeing, snorkeling equipment hire will cost extra.

Ferries to Fitzroy Island depart daily at about 9 AM and return to Cairns at around 5 PM. Home to clown fish, sea turtles and both soft and hard corals, the reef is very close to the beach. Shacks along the beach rent out snorkeling gear, paddleboards, paddle skis, kayaks, and more. You can also embark on a glass bottom tour which provides the perfect viewing opportunity to spot corals, turtles and colourful tropical fish swimming in their natural habitat. Running for about 30 minutes, these tours operate twice a day at 11 AM and 2 PM.

CAIRNS & THE GREAT BARRIER REEF TRAVEL GUIDE

While you are here, do walk up to the lighthouse on the island. Walking is relatively easy and the lighthouse is accessible. You can take spectacular photographs from the 260 meters high summit. Take the walking and hiking trails to view some of the best mangroves, woodlands, pristine rainforest greenery and coral beaches. Information related to the length of the track, time taken, directions etc. are available from the Fitzroy Island National Park Information center. From the *Boulder Lookout* track, a 300 meter track that can be covered in 30 minutes, to the *Summit Track*, a 2.6 kilometer track that takes about 3 hours, Fitzroy Island has walking tracks that cater to all ages and levels of fitness.

For those wanting to stay on the island overnight, take a look at Fitzroy Campgrounds. The cost per campsite is

$29 per night. Campgrounds include BBQ facilities, picnic tables, showers and toilets. You would have to arrange your own food and water. It is recommended that you call ahead to make a booking as sites are limited.

🌐 Cape Tribulation

Located only 45 minutes away from Port Douglas, Cape Tribulation is the village where the Daintree Rainforest meets the Great Barrier Reef. Cape Tribulation is one of the most unique rainforests in the world and new plant and animal species continue to be discovered here. A natural wonder, Cape Tribulation is home to species of plants that represent their evolution through 400 million years of life on this planet. Home to over 3,000 species of flora including some of the world's smallest and largest cycads and tree ferns, Cape Tribulation's nocturnal activities are best enjoyed during summer.

CAIRNS & THE GREAT BARRIER REEF TRAVEL GUIDE

Getting to Cape Tribulation is easy if you drive north from Port Douglas for about 45 minutes to the only cable ferry in Australia. The Daintree ferry provides access to the lowland rainforest. Package tours also depart from Port Douglas on a daily basis. These tours offer insights into some of the most hidden secrets of the rainforest which you might otherwise miss.

Visitors can explore the area by foot, on horseback, by river cruise or by kayak. For those who are adventurous at heart, you can even zip line through the rainforest, jungle surf or race through the rainforest on a 4WD vehicle. While you are in Cape Tribulation, do not miss the exotic fruit tasting events held at one of the local fruit farms.

 Cape York

The 4-hour drive from Cairns north to Cape York in a 4WD vehicle is considered one of Queensland's most adventurous activities. Take a scenic drive along the coast or a rugged inland drive through the rainforest. You can also combine your drive with a scenic flight or heli-ride on your return for the ultimate, 360-degree wilderness experience.

The inland route follows the Mulligan highway and has several lookouts along the way that offer spectacular views of lush plateaus and hillsides. Watch out for livestock as animals tend to wander onto the highways. On the other hand, the coastal route follows the Captain Cook Highway driving via Port Douglas, Mossman Gorge and Cape Tribulation. You can then follow the Bloomfield

Track along the Daintree coast, through Aborigine communities all the way to Cape York and Cooktown.

4WD vehicles are available for self-hire in Cairns. Alternatively, you can join one of the Cairns to Cape York 4WD guided tours. Coaches also operate on a regular basis between Cairns and Cooktown.

A cultural highlight, the Laura dance festival, is held in Cape York twice yearly. For those who are interested in exploring the Aborigine culture, the Alice Desert Festival held every September features art, music and dance.

🌏 Tully River White Water Rafting

Considered one of the best rafting rivers in Australia, the Tully River winds through world heritage rainforests and offers up to Grade 4 rapids. Often regarded as Australia's best one-day whitewater rafting experience, the Tully River winds through 45 rapids. Tour operators offer rafting trips of up to 5 hours.

Located 140 kilometers south of Cairns, the drive to Tully River is a scenic drive by coastal mountains, clear streams and rivers, sugarcane fields and exotic fruit farms. Rafting in Northern Queensland benefits from the year round tropical climate, pleasant water temperatures, and easy access to breathtaking scenery and gorge rapids. With exotic names like the Wet and Moisty Rapids, Alarm Clock Rapids, Staircase Rapids, and the Theatre Rapids, the Tully River rafting experience is highly recommended when visiting the Cairns area.

CAIRNS & THE GREAT BARRIER REEF TRAVEL GUIDE

Several tour operators offer additional add-ons at the end of a rafting trip including cliff diving, swimming the rapids and raft surfing. Tour operators provide the necessary rafting gear (life jacket, spray jacket, and helmet). Make sure you wear laced shoes that you can tie up tightly. Also, do carry along a swimsuit and a towel. Tour operators usually prefer that you be in your swimsuit by the time they pick you up at the starting point. A spare change of clothes is good to carry along, as is sunscreen.

Most tour operators split the daylong rafting experience with lunch. A BBQ lunch is included in most packages and the famed Ponytail Falls is often the location chosen for the barbecue. Here you will often dine with rafters from other tour packages. Photos taken by professional photographers will be available for purchase at the end of your rafting experience.

CAIRNS & THE GREAT BARRIER REEF TRAVEL GUIDE

Several tour operators offer pick up options from Cairns or from the hotels along the northern beaches. If you are driving, rafting operators will meet you directly at Tully. A pickup together with the rafting experience costs about $200 per person depending on the tour package. The rafting experience by itself costs about $150.

Several tour operators offer combo-packages including both skydiving and river rafting.

🌐 Aboriginal Cultural Tjapukai Tour

http://www.tjapukai.com.au/

Tjapukai is the aboriginal word for 'Rainforest' and the Aboriginal Cultural Tjapukai tour provides you an insight

CAIRNS & THE GREAT BARRIER REEF TRAVEL GUIDE

into the story of the Tjapukai people. Visitors watch theatre performances, engage in interactive activities and learn about the traditional customs of the aboriginal tribe. Starting off with a welcome drink, a traditional Tjapukai cultural show is followed by dinner. Kids can learn to throw spears and boomerangs, learn to play the didgeridoo, learn local tribal dances and take a part in the Tjapukai culture. Dramatic nighttime ceremonies by the lakeside complete the experience. Tjapukai Night Tours cost about $99 per adult and $50 per child. Family packages are also available for about $250. Transfers from Cairns or from the resorts along the northern beaches cost extra.

Tjapukai Culture Day tours are also available and cost about $35 per adult and $18 per child. Family packages are available for $90. Day tours include didgeridoo shows, theatre and magic shows.

The onsite Boomerang Restaurant offers morning and afternoon tea, light snacks as well as buffet lunches. You can browse in the adjoining gift shop to purchase indigenous souvenirs.

Budget Tips

 Accommodation

Cairns Coconut Holiday Resort

51 Anderson Road, Cairns, Queensland 4870, Australia

Tel: +61 7 4054 6644

http://www.coconut.com.au/

Formerly known as Cairns Coconut Caravan Resort, the family friendly resort offers self-contained accommodation

CAIRNS & THE GREAT BARRIER REEF TRAVEL GUIDE

along with a host of free activities including a splash park, resort pools, mini golf and more.

The winner of the 2010 Australian Tourism award in the Category 'Best Tourism and Holiday Park', the resort is located 6 kilometers away from the heart of the city. The average price is $120 per night.

Tropical Heritage Cairns

8 Minnie Street, Cairns,

Queensland 4870, Australia

Tel: +61 1800 212 212

http://www.heritagecairns.com.au/

Situated within walking distance from the Esplanade and the shopping mall, the resort offers several modern amenities like flat screen TVs, rental cars, bikes, Wi-Fi internet and more. Facilities include a pool, a BBQ area, bar and a gazebo with lounge. Rooms are priced at about $100 per night.

Atherton Hinterland Motel

44 Cook Street, Atherton,

Queensland 4883, Australia

Tel: +61 7 4091 3311

http://www.athertonhinterlandmotel.com.au/

Located within 10 minutes of walking distance from restaurants, cafes, bars and shops, the Atherton Hinterland Motel is built over 10,000 square metres of land that offer you a spectacular view of the hillside and the creeks. The site has a free BBQ area that can be used by guests. The hotel also offers sumptuous breakfast all seven days of the week. Accommodation is priced at $100 a night.

Port Douglas Motel

9 Davidson St, Port Douglas,

Queensland, Australia

Tel: +61 7 4099 5248

http://www.portdouglasmotel.com.au/

Located within 2 minutes walking distance to the beach and within only 200 metres of shops, bars and restaurants, the recently refurbished Port Douglas Motel is a 4 star motel experience at an affordable price. With all modern amenities, Port Douglas Motel rooms are priced at $110 per night.

🌏 Restaurants, Cafés & Bars

Bayleaf Balinese Restaurant

Corner of Lake & Gatton Street,

Cairns, Queensland 4870, Australia

Tel: +61 07 40514622

http://www.bayvillage.com.au/bayleaf

Offering authentic flavours of the tropical Balinese cuisine, Bayleaf is one of the most talked-about restaurants in Cairns. Open for lunch from 12 to 2 PM and for dinner from 6 PM till date, the restaurant offers scrumptious delicacies at affordable prices.

Appetizers are priced from $12 - $18 while authentic main course dishes are priced at $20 - $35.

Houdini's Gourmet Pizza

Shop 2/375 Sheridan Street,

Cairns, Queensland 4871, Australia

Tel: +61 07 4041 0742

http://houdinispizza.com/

Away from the readymade standard-ingredient pizzas, Houdini's Gourmet Pizza offers authentic, made to order pizzas using exotic vegetables and fragrant spices. With ingredients like artichoke hearts, Spanish onions, spicy chorizo and roasted pumpkin, the gourmet pizzas offered here are very different than those at Dominos or Pizza Hut. The restaurant also offers standard pizzas using regular ingredients for those who like to play it safe. Offered in the price range of $ 25 - $40, Houdini's

Gourmet Pizza is a good option for those who are looking for something different.

Grill'd

77 The Esplanade, Cairns,

Queensland 4870, Australia

Tel: +61 07 4041 4200

http://www.grilld.com.au/

Grill'd is for those who crave home food and would like to be reminded every once in a while of how it is back home. It is also an excellent option if you are short of time and need to pick up some gourmet fast food for the road. Offering steak and grilled meats in the Wild West fashion, Grill'd is famous for its hot burgers – be it beef, chicken or lamb. For the vegetarian eater, Grill'd also offers vegetarian dishes. Priced at around $12 - $15, Grill'd is affordable and well liked by the locals.

Devine Gelato

Shop 3/5 Aplin Street,

Cairns, Queensland4870, Australia

Tel: +61 07 4041 4959

No meal is complete without dessert. Enter Devine Gelato, a small eatery that boasts of the best dessert – ice cream, sorbets and gelato – in Cairns. Stated to be eerily similar to gelato available only in Florence, Italy, Devine Gelato offers homemade authentic sorbets, gelatos and ice creams. Priced at low prices ranging from just $3, Devine Gelato is considered a must-visit eatery and lends a perfectly sweet ending to your Cairns visit.

🌐 Shopping

The Pier

Pier Point Rd, Cairns,

Queensland 4870, Australia

Tel: +61 07 4051 7244

www.thepier.com.au

Offering a beautiful view over the marina and its spectacular blue waters, the Pier is an excellent place to shop for international and Australian designer brands and you will be able to find products that fit every budget. The Pier also hosts a number of restaurants offering a range of cuisines from around the world.

Cairns Central

Corner of McLeod and Spence Streets,

Cairns, Queensland 4870

Tel: +61 07 4041 4111

www.cairnscentral.com.au

With over 180 stores, Cairns Central is the largest shopping district in northern Queensland. Though the center is open seven days of the week, individual stores maintain their own opening and closing hours. The food court, offering multi-cuisine food, is the perfect way to end the evening after a day of shopping.

Know Before You Go

🌏 Entry Requirements

With the exception of New Zealand, nationals of most countries will need a valid passport and a visa when travelling to Australia. Upon arrival, you will also be required to fill out a passenger card, which includes a declaration regarding your health and character. A tourist visa is usually valid for 6 months, but can be extended for another 6 months. If travelling to Australia for business reasons, you will want to look into the requirements for a short term or long term business visas. The former is valid for up to 3 months, while the latter is valid for up to 4 years, but requires sponsorship from an Australian company.

🌏 Health Insurance

If visiting Australia from a country that has a reciprocal health care agreement with Australia, you will be able to use Medicare - Australia's public health insurance - for the duration of your stay. Participating countries include Ireland, New Zealand, Italy, Sweden, Norway, Slovenia, Belgium, Finland, the Netherlands and the UK. However, this only covers emergency care and limits you to using public hospitals. Visitors on a student visa from Norway, Finland, Malta and the Republic of Ireland may require additional cover and visitors who do not have access to Medicare will be required, as part of their visa application, to obtain adequate healthcare for the duration of their stay in Australia. To extend your cover, Overseas Visitors Health Cover (OVHC) can be arranged through a number of Australian health fund companies. Additional health insurance is mandatory if visiting on a long stay working visa. There are no required vaccinations for entering Australia, but a booster shot for tetanus and diphtheria will be a good idea, if your last vaccination was more than ten years ago. If travelling from Southeast Asia, you may want to get a shot for Hepatitis A and B, as well as typhoid.

🌏 Travelling with Pets

Nearly all dogs and cats travelling to Australia will need to spend some time in quarantine, but the duration depends on the country of origin. The only countries exempt from this requirement is New Zealand, Cocos Island and Norfolk Island. The minimum quarantine period is 10 days and to qualify for this, your pet will need to be tested for rabies 6 months prior to your travel date. The cost for quarantine and customs clearance is approximately $1,800AUD. You will need to apply for an

CAIRNS & THE GREAT BARRIER REEF TRAVEL GUIDE

import permit for your pet. If travelling from a non-approved country such as Russia, India, Sri Lanka and the Philippines, your pet will need to spend 6 months in an approved country and be tested for rabies prior to being allowed entry in Australia. Approved countries include Antigua & Barbuda, Argentina, Austria, the Bahamas, Belgium, Bermuda, the British Virgin Islands, Brunei, Bulgaria, Canada, the Canary and Balearic Islands, the Cayman Islands, Chile, the Republic of Croatia, the Republic of Cyprus, the Czech Republic, Denmark, Finland, France, Germany, Gibraltar, Greece, Greenland, Guernsey, Hong Kong, Hungary, Ireland, the Isle of Man, Israel, Italy, Jamaica, Jersey, Kuwait, Latvia, Lithuania, Luxembourg, Macau, Malta, parts of Malaysia (Peninsular, Sabah and Sarawak only), Monaco, Montenegro, the Netherlands, Netherlands—Antilles & Aruba, Norway, Poland, Portugal, Puerto Rico, Qatar, Reunion, Saipan, Serbia, Seychelles, Slovakia, Slovenia, South Africa, South Korea, Spain, St Kitts and Nevis, St Lucia, St Vincent & the Grenadines, Sweden, Switzerland (including Liechtenstein), Taiwan, Trinidad and Tobago, the United Arab Emirates, the United Kingdom, the United States, Northern Mariana Islands, Puerto Rico and the US Virgin Islands as well as American Samoa, Bahrain, Barbados, Christmas Island, Cook Island, the Falkland Islands, the Federated States of Micronesia, Fiji, French Polynesia, Guam, Hawaii, Iceland, Japan, Kiribati Mauritius, Nauru, New Caledonia, Niue, Palau, Papua New

Guinea, Samoa, Singapore, the Solomon Islands, the Kingdom of Tonga, Tuvalu, Vanuatu and the Futuna Islands. There are quarantine stations in Sydney and Melbourne. A quarantine period can be waived in the case of service dog, provided that proper documented evidence of the dog's status is submitted, but in this case, the dog will need to be inspected upon arrival by an approved veterinarian and supervised for the 10 day period immediately after entry. You are not allowed to bring certain dog breeds such as the Dogo Argentino, Fila Brazileiro, Japanese Tosa, Pit Bull Terrier, American Pit Bull, Perro de Presa Canario or Presa Canario into Australia. Other animals that cannot be brought into Australia are chinchillas, fish, ferrets, guinea pigs, hamsters, lizards, mice, snakes, spiders and turtles. In the case of avian species, only birds originating from New Zealand are allowed.

Airports

Sydney Airport (SYD) is located just 8km south of Sydney's central business district and serves as the primary gateway for international air traffic into Australia. It is the country's busiest airport and provides connections to New Zealand, Singapore, Hong Kong, Dubai, Japan, the USA and Malaysia. Domestically, it also provides access to the country's six main states, as well as to Tasmania. The second busiest airport is

Melbourne Airport (MEL). It is located about 23km from the central business area of Melbourne, but this is easy to reach via the Skybus Super Shuttle, which connects to the city's public transport network at the Southern Cross station. Melbourne Airport welcomes international flights from the Far East, the Middle East and the USA and also connects to Australia's top domestic destinations. The busiest airport in Queensland is **Brisbane Airport** (BNE), which provides connections to over 40 domestic destinations and over 25 international destinations. Other important airports in Queensland are the **Gold Coast Airport** (OOL) and the **Cairns Airport** (CNS). As the 4th busiest airport, **Perth Airport** (PER) serves as a gateway to Western Australia. **Adelaide Airport** (ADL) is the most important airport in the Southern Territory of Australia, while **Darwin Airport** (DRW), one of the oldest airports in Australia, opens up the Northern Territory. **Canberra Airport** (CBR) provides access to the capital. Tasmania is served by **Hobart International Airport** (HBA) in Hobart.

Airlines

Qantas Airways is the third oldest airline in the world. It was founded in 1920 through the efforts of two Australian Flying Corps veterans, W Hudson Fysh and Paul McGinness. The enterprise pioneered a series of milestones, starting with the

CAIRNS & THE GREAT BARRIER REEF TRAVEL GUIDE

establishment of an airmail service, the Flying Doctor Service, a regular connection between Brisbane and Darwin and the addition of international destinations such as Singapore. Qantas was an early adapter to the benefits of Boeing jumbo jets and one of the first airlines to establish a trans-Pacific route. Today it is Australia's national flag carrier and the country's largest airline. Qantas is a partner of the OneWorld Air Alliance, connecting it with British Airlines, Iberia, Japan Airlines, Finnair, LAN Airlines and Sri Lankan Airlines.

Qantas has a founding interest in Australia's budget service, Jetstar Airways, which is based at Melbourne Airport. Together with Qantas, Jetstar oversees Jetstar Asia Airways, Jetstar Pacific Airlines and Jetstar Japan. Qantas also operates a regional brand, QantasLink, which harnesses the combined coverage of Eastern Australian Airlines, Sunstate Airlines and Southern Australia Airlines to provide a regional and domestic service. Eastern Australia Airlines was founded late in the 1940s, when it served mainly to connect remote rural communities under the name Tamair. During the mid-1980s, it was acquired by Australian Airlines, who in turn sold it to Qantas in 1992.

After Qantas, Virgin Australia is the second largest airline. Founded under the Virgin brand by Richard Branson and Brett Godfrey in 2000, the company expanded rapidly after

September 2001 to fill the gap left by the demise of Ansett Australia. Virgin Australia is in partnership with the regional service SkyWest Airlines as well as Air New Zealand and the US carrier Delta. Additionally, it operates the budget airline, Tigerair Australia as a subsidiary of Virgin Australia. Tigerair offers connections to 11 domestic destinations as well as nearby Bali.

West Wing Aviation is a domestic service based in Queensland and manages connections to smaller and more remote destinations within Queensland. Airnorth was founded in the late 1970s. Based in Darwin, it provides a regional service that covers the northern part of Australia. King Island Airlines offers connections between Moorabbin, near Melbourne and King Island, Tasmania.

Hubs

Sydney Airport serves as the primary hub for Qantas Air. Qantas also uses Melbourne Airport, Brisbane Airport, Perth Airport and Adelaide Airport as hubs. Virgin Australia uses Brisbane Airport, Melbourne Airport and Sydney Airport as hubs, but also has a strong presence at Adelaide Airport, Perth Airport and Gold Coast Airport. Additionally, Melbourne Airport serves as hub for the Virgin subsidiary Tigerair, as well as Jetstar Airlines. Darwin International Airport serves as a primary hub for Airnorth. West Wing Aviation uses Townsville Airport in Queensland as hub. Brisbane Airport serves as a hub for Sunstate Airlines.

Money Matters

Currency

The currency of Australia is the Australian dollar. Notes are issued in denominations of $5, $10, $20, $50 and $100. Coins are issued in denominations of 5 cents, 10 cents, 20 cents and 50 cents as well as $1 and $2.

Banking/ATMs

ATM machines are widely distributed across Australia in both urban and rural locations. Besides bank lobbies, they are often found in shopping centers, service stations, convenience stores and pubs. You should be able to use bank cards that are part of the Cirrus, Plus or Maestro networks. Most ATMs will explicitly indicate which cards are accepted. Using a debit card is fairly easy in Australia, but many ATMs will charge an additional fee of $2 or more for non-customers. There are exceptions. As the Westpac banking group is partnered with several overseas banks including Bank of America, Scotia Bank and Barclays, customers of those banks will be exempted from the banking fee. An alternative to using your bank card is the Travelex Cash Passport, an easy-to-use prepaid card which can be topped up using your debit card.

Credit Cards

MasterCard and Visa are widely accepted throughout Australia, while Diners Club and American Express will also be legal tender at larger shops and chain stores. Some shops will decline credit cards for purchases under AUS$15 and surcharges may apply for some businesses. Until recently, credit card users in Australia had the choice of using a PIN or signature as security for credit card transactions, but from August 2016, PIN-enabled cards will be mandatory. You should make sure that your credit card is compatible with this new policy. Also remember to advise your bank or credit card of your travel plans prior to your departure.

🌐 Tourist Tax

From July 2016, working backpackers will be taxed at 32.5 percent on their Australian income.

🌐 Claiming Back VAT

Visitors to Australia can obtain a refund on purchases of at least $300, spent at a single business. Residents of the Australia's External Territories - the Norfolk Islands, Christmas Island and the Cocos (Keeling) Islands - also qualify for a refund from GST paid under the Tourist Refund Scheme (TRS). To obtain a refund, you must present valid documentation of your purchases in the form of a tax invoice or sales receipt at an international airport or seaport when departing Australia and this should happen within 60 days of making those purchases. You should keep the goods handy within your hand luggage, to have it available for inspection. To save time, download the TRS app where you can enter details electronically and use a specially dedicated shortcut queue to process your claim.

Tipping Policy

In Australia, restaurants are required by law to pay their waiting staff a working wage and tipping is not really expected, although the influence of tourism as well as American culture has influenced Australian attitudes in recent years. In high-end restaurants, roughly half of the diners might be expected to leave a tip and in big cities, it will be more common to tip. If service is good and you want to show your appreciation, 10 percent is regarded as fair and sufficient. It is not common practice to tip in hotels and in casinos, tipping is forbidden. In bars, it is accepted practice to tell the bartender to keep the change. The same applies to cab drivers.

Connectivity

Mobile Phones

Australia uses the GSM mobile network, which means that it should be compatible with phones from the UK or the European Union, but may be incompatible with phones from the USA and Canada. If you are able to use Australian networks, you will still face the high charges levied for international roaming. There is an alternative. If your phone is unlocked, you will be able to replace your own SIM card with an Australian SIM card for the duration of your stay.

Australia has 3 basic mobile networks - Telstra, Vodafone and Optus. Telstra offers the best coverage of Australia's rural and more remote locations, but is also one of the more expensive operators. If you plan to stick to urban locations, the coverage offered by Optus and Vodafone might be sufficient for your needs. Telstra sim cards are available at $2, with recharge packages starting at $20. Data only packages are priced at between $30 and $50. Optus sim cards begin at $2 for just the sim, with top-ups priced at between $10 and $50. Vodafone pre-paid sim cards begin at $1 for just the sim, with data packages priced at between $3 and $15. For a super budget option, consider the deals offered by the reseller Amaysim, which also offers the option to pay for top-ups online, via PayPal.

 Dialling Code

The dialling code for Australia is +61.

Emergency Numbers

General emergency: 000

Text Emergency Relay Service: 106

MasterCard: 1800 120 113

Visa: 1800 450 346

General Information

Public Holidays

1 January: New Year's Day

26 January: Australia Day

March/April: Good Friday

March/April: Easter Monday

25 April: Anzac Day

23 June: The Queen's Birthday

25 December: Christmas

26 December: Boxing Day

There are various holidays that are celebrated at state level or within certain religious communities.

🌐 Time Zones

The Australian continent is divided into three different time zones. The eastern states of Queensland, Victoria and New South Wales, as well as the Australian Capital Territory and Tasmania fall under Australian East Standard Time (AEST), which can be calculated as Greenwich Mean Time/Co-ordinated Universal Time (GMT/UTC) +10. Australian Central Standard Time (ACST) is used in the Northern Territory, South Australia and in the town of Broken Hill, which is found in the western part of New South Wales. Australian Central Standard Time can be calculated as Greenwich Mean Time/Co-ordinated Universal Time (GMT/UTC) +9 and a half hour. Western Australia uses Australian Western Standard time, which can be calculated as Greenwich Mean Time/Co-ordinated Universal Time (GMT/UTC) +8.

🌐 Daylight Savings Time

For Daylight Savings Time, clocks are set forward by one hour at 2am on the first Sunday in October and set back one hour at 3am on the first Sunday in April. Queensland, Western Australia and the Northern Territory do not observe Daylight Savings Time.

🌏 School Holidays

In Australia, the academic year runs from January to December. Generally, schools open towards the end of January or very early in February. There is a 2 to 3 week break from the end of March or early in April, a winter vacation in June/July and a 2 week spring break in September or October. The summer vacation is usually from mid December to the end of January. Exact dates are set by the state authority in question and may vary.

🌏 Trading Hours

Trading hours are set at state rather than national level, but in most states there are little or no restrictions on hours. Generally, shopping hours in Australia are from 8am to 9pm on weekdays, 8am to 5.30pm on Saturdays and 9am to 6pm on Sundays. Most non-essential businesses will be closed on ANZAC Day, Good Friday and Christmas Day. In South Australia, trade on Sundays and Public Holidays are restricted to the hours between 11am and 5pm. In Queensland, most shopping centers close at 5pm, but will stay open for late trade on one day of the week. In Western Australia, large businesses and chain stores are restricted to trading between 9am and 5pm from Monday to

Saturday and between 11am and 5pm on Sundays and Public Holidays.

🌐 Driving Policy

Australians drive on the left hand side of the road. In most states, you will be able to drive on a foreign licence, provided that it is valid and that an English translation (or International Driver's Licence) is available. The minimum driving age varies from 16 years and 6 months in the Northern Territory to 18 in Victoria, but in most states it is 17 years. The speed limit is 60km per hour for cities and urban areas, 50km per hour in suburban areas and 110km per hour on highways and rural roads. Laws regarding texting and the use of cell phones while driving vary, but in most states, a hands-free kit is required. Learner drivers or inexperienced drivers are not allowed to handle their phones at all while driving. The legal limit for drinking and driving is a Blood Alcohol Concentration (BAC) of 0.05%, but learner drivers and inexperienced drivers are not allowed to drink at all when driving.

Drinking Policy

In Australia, the minimum drinking age is 18. Children under the age of 18 are only allowed on licenced premises, if accompanied by a parent. Only businesses with a liquor licence are allowed to supply alcohol to the public and by law, they are required to ask customers and patrons for some form of identification. Local councils in Australia have the power to declare an area a dry zone, which means that no alcohol may be consumed there. The ban may relate to a particular event or can apply on an ongoing basis.

Smoking Policy

In the early 1990s, Australia introduced legislation to restrict smoking in public places. Smoking is banned in restaurants, bars and licenced clubs, although there are designated smoking areas. Recently, the ban was widened to include smoking in vehicles with children under the age of 18. Smoking is also forbidden in outdoor play areas for children, at swimming pools, bus stops and railway stations. In New South Wales, you may not smoke within 4m of a building entrance and in Western Australia, smoking is prohibited in the patrolled areas of beaches. All tobacco products are required by law to carry health warnings.

🌐 Electricity

Electricity: 230 volts

Frequency: 50 Hz

Australia's electricity sockets are compatible with the Type I plugs, a plug that features three rectangular pins or prongs, arranged in a triangular shape, with two of the pins set at opposing angles to each other. They are similar to the plugs and sockets used in Fiji. If travelling from the USA or Canada, you will also need a power converter or transformer to convert the voltage from 230 to 110, to avoid damage to your appliances. The latest models of certain types of camcorders, cell phones and digital cameras are dual-voltage, which means that they were manufactured with a built in converter, but you will have to consult your electronics dealer about that.

🌐 Food & Drink

When they have the time for a hearty breakfast, Australians love a fry-up similar to the full English breakfast with eggs, bacon, sausage, mushroom and baked beans. Other popular breakfast options include porridge, cereal and milk or simply a slice of toast with vegemite - that is Australia's twist on good old Marmite. Technically, Australia lies in the Orient and a robust community of Asian immigrants has ensured the enduring popularity of Asian cuisine. Australia also sometimes offers exotic game, in the form of kangaroo, emu and crocodile steak. Adventurous diners will want to sample bush food, but it is not for the faint of heart. Bush tucker originated with the hunter-gatherer lifestyle of Australia's Aboriginal people and incorporates a variety of home-grown fruits and vegetables, as well as edible seeds and insects. One of the best known delicacies is the witchetty grub, which can be eaten raw or cooked. Other indigenous staples include bush yam, bush banana, conkleberries and wattle seeds.

In Australia, beer is serious business, complete with its own lingo of buzz phrases. Australians refer to a can as a "tinnie", a case of 24 cans as a "slab" and a bottle of beer as a "brownie" or, in the case of a long-necked bottle, as a "tally". While a short-necked bottle is called a "stubby", do not mistake it with a "Darwin stubby", the Northern Territory variety with a 2.25 litre capacity. Even glasses are divided into "pints", "schooners", "middys" or "pots", according to size, and you should say "My shout" to announce your intention to buy the next round.

The most popular beer brands in Australia are VB (Victoria Bitter) and Castlemaine's XXXX Gold and other beers worth

CAIRNS & THE GREAT BARRIER REEF TRAVEL GUIDE

sampling include Carlton Draught, Toohey's Extra Dry, Hahn Premium Light, Crown Lager, Pure Blonde and James Boag's Premium. In Queensland and New South Wales, Bundeberg beer is another favorite. Australia has a robust wine industry, of which the best known export is Penfolds Grange. Other well established wineries are Wolf Blass, Lindemans, Rosemount, Jacob's Creek, Yalumba, Berri Estates, Yellowglen and Hardy Wine Co. Tasmania produces top notch whiskies, such as the award-winning Sullivan's Cove and great cider, such as Red Sails, Lost Pippin and Pagan Cider. When it comes to soft drinks, Coca-Cola rules. Australia's taste for coffee has been influenced by the significant community of Italian immigrants. Visiting techno-geeks can try the newly launched Smartcup, an Australian invention which can be linked to a CafePay app and lets you pay for your daily brew online.

 Useful Websites

http://www.australia.com/en
http://wikitravel.org/en/Australia
https://www.australianexplorer.com/
http://www.downundr.com/tips-and-tricks/top-ten-destinations
http://www.britz.com.au/
http://www.driveaustralia.com.au/suggested-routes/
http://ozyroadtripper.com.au/

CAIRNS & THE GREAT BARRIER REEF TRAVEL GUIDE

http://australiaroadtrip.co.uk/

https://www.ozexperience.com/

Printed in Great Britain
by Amazon